SEA DRUMS

& Other Poems

Bert J. Hubinger

ROSEBUD PRESS
TRAPPE, MARYLAND USA

An Imprint of
EASTWIND PUBLISHING

Library of Congress Control Number: 2003091552

ISBN   1-885457-50-2

Published by
ROSEBUD PRESS
an Imprint of Eastwind Publishing
Annapolis & Trappe, Maryland USA

Cover photo by the author

Printed in United States

For Shelley

CONTENTS

◆

ACKNOWLEDGEMENTS

I wish to thank the following publications in which many of these poems have previously appeared or will appear:

American Poetry Anthology; Blue Unicorn; Cabin Fever: Poets at Joaquin Miller's Cabin, 1984-2001; CQ: California State Poetry Quarterly; Caveat (Golden Gate University); *The Cormorant* (Oceanic Society); *Draconian Measures* (Zenith Beast); *Earthwise Literary Calendar; Folio* (American University); *A Galaxy of Verse; The Galley Sail Review; Heaven in My Heart* (National Arts Society); *Hoosier Challenger; The Kindred Spirit; Lucky Star* (Erie Street Press); *Manna; Maryland Poetry Review; The Noe Valley Voice; New Voices: an Anthology of California Poets* (Small Poetry Press); *Paroles* (Dartmouth College); *Peaceful Reveries* (The Poetry Guild); *The Plowman Anthology; Poetic Voices of America* (Sparrowgrass Poetry); *Poets On: Arrivals; Prophetic Voices; Ripples; Riverrun; Santa Clara Review; Sequoia* (Stanford Literary Magazine); *Social Anarchism; The Sounds of Poetry* (The National Library of Poetry); *Unknowns* (Abri Publications); *Visions* (Black Buzzard Press); *World of Poetry Anthology;* and *Writer's Gazette* (Trouvere).

SEA DRUMS

The Deciduous Advantage

Hiking through the woods above a sequin
Bay, we marvel at the deciduous advantage;
Red-tipped fingers claw at the sun.
Below the first March buds, near water's edge,

Squirrels and birds rummage through last year's
Transparent leaves. Most trees,
Still bare, crack the sky, still standing their winter
Watch; but soon branches will release

A fury of flowers, fruits and seeds, new growth
From old limbs. A ragged nest, improbably
Perched in the lacy crown of a tall oak,
Seems to float in blue. These woods defy

Cold death, by succumbing to it, by baring all,
Having shed solar sails like old skin;
Their parchment hands cover the earth. How well
This empty mesh holds life's horizon!

Soon tall poplars will hide nests and sky,
Their dark web clothed in extravagant green;
What prodigal skeletons these are, patiently
Waiting their turn to live again.

Nancy Reagan Looks to the East and Turns to Salt

Even as she waves,
she whitens, crystalline
the fingers, block-like
stumps the legs.
Nancy now becomes
her porcelain,
looking back toward
Kremlin walls.
Advisers warned, don't
look back,
ratings will crumble,
dynasties fall. Yeats
revives and moans,
Our god is dust, our
God is prisoner of
special interest. But
once in a while we hear
from the past. Don't
look back. You will
surely turn to salt,
and cows will lick
your monument.
The face is blurred,
melting, returning to
the sea. You will never
wonder how it happened,
never see or hear
the lone humpback
or great white sperm
beating up against the bland
actors, laughing at their
loose portrayals, their

unconvincing roles.
The whale cruises
up the delta searching for
the source. The source is
ours. Even a parasite
knows how to find it,
up the river,
beyond the salt.

The Escalator at the Civic Center

Phoenicians would have shipped oars
and set sail for the horizon; I merely
stepped on a subway escalator, going up.
I'd been told this escalator would take me
to the top, that it was aimed at quasars,
the most distant, glittering edge
of the universe, the light beyond the light.

With supernova power, I would rise
above the infinite blackness of the subway,
on a real stairway to the stars,
trillions of nutrinos riddling me
as I rode on the escalator of the gods,
writing poems on the sides of passing ships,
while gorillas below attacked the trains.

But instead of escalating, I just stood still;
the escalator was broken, motionless,
and whatever heights its supple steel
might have reached, it didn't.
All over the earth, the escalators froze,
like flowing lava that's hardened into rock,
like stairs that suddenly go nowhere.

Soon nothing moved, and the people themselves
hardened into stone, one by one slipping
back into the black void, each dark mass
bowed down as if to say, Good night,
my fellow commuters; we're the people
who just got off the last train.
We're the people waiting to be escalated.

The Catalyst

Who knows how these chain reactions
Flash down our histories
And spread their heat

Who cares? I only know
This ancient mariner
Plunges through your perfect seas
Unchanged and yet forever changed

Who knows how it could happen
Beyond the ancillary catalysts
Of those before, how mad
Freewheeling molecules could intertwine

Through and through? I only know
These ironic elements
And compound energies of mine
Love only you

Blue Crab Blues

Native estuary born,
flesh inside bone, you are claw
and paddle, flattened abdomen;
the song of the shallows
echoes inside your chitinous skin.
Tail filled with black eyes — hostile,
bitter — you are destined for deeper mud,
where few survivors go.
Obviously you were a mistake;
but hope is the mother of all crabs,
and thousands escape your brown sponge,
a cloud of larvae in brackish hues,
relentless, mechanical legs churning,
compound eyes locked on stalks,
antennae trembling with planktonic passion.
Who will see this struggle among so many
cold-blooded hunters and prey,
glazed eyes like pitiless, dying suns,
life filtered through decay?
Through a tide of war, new claws
pinch their hard-won detritus;
walls breached, shells replaced, casualties
slide along planes of crab memory,
dissolving in the slow current,
flowing toward the sea.

The Jellyfish

Unmanned by those plankton memories
I swim across the ocean of current events
into the primordial past, stinging
my enemies, my food—
your face, coiled and barbed,
springs into my eyes
like a mad embryo:

So much to throw away.
Our mouths, laughing in salt,
sing those special fears, those
lovely songs from windy skeletons
like snow falling in the sea.

Unmanned by one-celled passion,
I retreat down the food chain
like a wounded pelican,
a gull backing off
from a crab, webbed feet
slipping in lavender gel,
screaming at the waves
that chew our nerves;
the foam holds certain details,
broken messages in long piles of weed.

Nowhere Else to Go

Poised on the brink
Of a backward, vertical race, I shrink
From the bright sun
Of a nameless cliff, barely begun
Yet somehow almost at the end
As if elastic line would send
My life into reverse
Falling, soaring, the end no worse
Than the beginning
The results all the same
Some kind of bouncing game
Peering over the edge
Of my days, balancing on the ledge
And ready for another dive
To somehow come alive
The cord, the plunge, the screams
The water as it seems
To rush up to meet me
Then the band yanking me free
Of gravity — they'll say I flew
Back up, into the past, with a new
Chance to hit tomorrow
Because there was nowhere else to go

Alone Late at Night
at the Beachcomber Motel, Naples, Florida

At 37, I am my mother's age,
too restless to float or swim,
in a small room under bright light,
asking her to help me now as she could
when she was just a girl, when we met
on that long beach, flowing like her hair,
like a frayed splinter locked inside my skin;

At 37, I try to put it all together:
the highway hissing and moaning,
my moon glaring through the windows,
my mother, who froze her age at 37,
and Van Gogh, who died in a small room
surrounded by yellow flowers
and the smell of fresh-baked pastry;

At 37, sharing my bed with the young moon,
I think of my mother, finally grown old,
swathed in the glowing robes of stars,
like strands of DNA slowly spiraling
out of reach, as she shines down
on this beach, on lovers wrapped in blankets,
who will live so easily without her.

Shelley

Listen carefully to the green hands
Of the yellow poplar
Quietly clapping in the hot breath
Of June:
I miss my wife.
Listen to the voice of summer
Blaring as if important:
Children coddled
In the busy traffic of the afternoon.
And all these warm days
Will soon cool in the bronze air:
Tall trees nod toward fall
Oak and sycamore, beech and sweetgum
Draped in dry vines.
Owl and crow
Echo through territories yet unknown
Curling into sleepless memory of her.

Too Marvelous for Words

I always wanted to be Bogart, at the end of "Dark Passage,"
waiting for Bacall in a cafe in Paita, on the coast of Peru.
Suddenly the band begins to play that ancient melody,
and there she is; and I'm dancing with her,
no longer bitter, flowing into an ocean of orchids
and last lines, above the glittering lights
of another long cape, another empty horizon.

She knows both of my faces, this angel
I knew would never return to my arms; but here she is,
and I struggle to the surface for some cause
other than survival, above the shallow harbor boats
winding through narrow mangrove cuts,
lost in their many branches, snagging a green limb
in the current, hanging in red roots.

No more silver flash of bonefish in the buzzing heat!
No more needlefish snapping on the flats, lost in the glades.
Only the twilight music of cicadas shrill droning,
wings drumming clear ripples in the sweet air
above a small bay; only the keys to a new jungle
growing in the sand, and the bold curve of her lips
smiling she wants to be there.

CatMan

You may pet me now
And then feed me
No that is enough stroking
I know you love me
But I want to go outside now
And if I am out
I want in
And then I want out again
I will always demand
And you will never understand
But sometimes I will let you love me
I stare at what you cannot see
I will never trust or need
But I will always return
As long as you feed me
And don't call me Tiger
Tigers are on their way out
I am the perfect survivor
The perfect hunter
I am *Felis catus*
I am the Autistic of God
You are my slave
And that is why I rub against you
I may even sleep with you
A cat, a coat, and a hunger
But always self-serving
Not cute, not cuddly

But a killer, with lightning knives
And I am much tougher than you
The kings and queens
Inside me scream and flog
But don't ever mistake me
For a dog

The Spruce Goose

She is the first
and last of her kind,
a white giant glowing
in the darkness of a giant dome,
wings spanning a football field,
tail rising toward a black ceiling
as far in the night sky
as the eye can see,
almost as high as her memory.
Howard Hughes took over her controls
and flew his vast wooden bird
just once, just above the waves,
in 1947.
Still in the cockpit, headset
permanently on, he picks up her voice
from the past, inside that dome,
in the glowing darkness
of that black and white time machine.
And she may speak the same language,
but she's not the same plane;
she may speak of yesterday,
of what is gone today,
but only Howard Hughes hears
what she has to say.
Inside that dome
under artificial night,
the Spruce Goose lies waiting,
hungry, ready for flight.

The Friendly Church on the Corner

Outside the Formosan Methodist
Church at Hudson and Manila, my father
is still alive, but I keep sinking,
walking the long circle around the city,
thinking, is that a Miami road,
and where is my car?
The road is wet and steaming
from last night's rain,
and the lady on the radio sings,
"I don't want to set the world on fire. . ."
and it's raining again, and I remember
driving in the rain in Miami,
my father trying to sing that song.
And we would shout him down, and laugh,
and his singing was really bad
and I wish I could hear it now.

The Perforator God

What foolish yearning stirs my old love,
what onshore breeze ripples the fetid surface,
gathering in the motley sailing craft,
the patient insects hovering
in the salty air,
in the golden weed floating toward the beach.
She had her years;
the skulls of spacecraft sing a hymn
to shining Canaveral;
but the sun slips from the palms
and the green light fades this afternoon
with the regular pulse of salty dogs barking
at some stubborn redneck;
the empty, darkening minds
whine in the late sun,
a last race of glistening spacecraft
waiting for the end of their day,
thinking there must be some way out of this.
I push too hard,
all the way back to the muscular love
under a red sun, locked in the strain
of her perfect legs,
all the way back to the beginning,
under a giant Olympic torch belching fire
in a race already lost;
my old love, with her golden thighs
and charged copper hair
screams at the breeze;
I fly across her Everglades in an airboat, her lips
roaring in my ears, her hair rushing
through my days, her face
simmering through the channel in the Keys,
through the burned scales of love,

the dark holes, the lucid aquamarine.
She had her years;
I come to her Florida sun
like a barracuda, a snapper,
all that salty past just a blur
of sawgrass blowing downwind like sweet surf.
I come to the sweet skin, the eager voice,
the melting tongue,
neither lunatic nor genius,
searching her curved surface for survivors.

Wall Dive

Half a mile off Cozumel, we back flip off the boat
into 85 degrees; thumbs point down;
we descend; visibility 100 feet.
Soon we're gliding over the bottom
with an overfed grouper; brain coral looms ahead,
rising from the depths.
   Air pressure 2800, time 5 minutes.
We enter a maze of canyons, caverns,
tunnels, huge tubes of fire red sponge;
suddenly we're hovering over the edge
of a cliff, and there's nothing below us,
or everything; light just falls away,
dissolving forever into layers
of aquamarine and cobalt blue;
we slip in and out of holes in a living reef stretching
thousands of years into the distance;
the surface is a glimmering sheet as we fin effortlessly
among undulating silver clouds
of grunt and jack and yellowtail snapper.
   Air 1500, time 20 minutes.
Queen angelfish ripple through the current
into tangles of elkhorn branches;
green moray eels spread their jaws;
we nod in passing to spines and claws, spots and stripes,
rainbow parrots, golden butterflies
darting gracefully among feather stars,
brilliant lives from another world;
we almost forget the regulator, free of time,
and depth, and fear, drifting with the glittering plankton;
how we yearn for our beginnings.

Air 600, time 40 minutes.
Thumbs point up; slowly, reluctantly,
we rise above the wall
toward the glistening surface,
our boat a dark wedge
slicing through a watery sky.

Buddy Breathing

You check regulators and BCDs, and stare
through masks like clumsy seals in neoprene;
you sink with lead belts, tanks and fins
to practice buddy breathing.
At fifty feet, watery sun still shines
through sea trees, golden-brown leaves of kelp
waving sinuously in the hazy blue surge
of Lover's Cove, Monterey Bay.
Thick stalks surround you, with spider crabs
and orange fish and banded shrimp,
bat rays and sea stars, and green anemones;
so many ancient forms of arms and legs and tentacles!
They almost seem to ignore you, dodging
through the kelp forest, among the tangled memories
of a distant time when you belonged below the surface,
when you could make love without such apparatus.
You kiss, sharing dangerous air, ready
to save each other in the underwater sun. She signals
"cut" with a hand across her throat,
and points to her mouth.
You inhale twice, and pass the mouthpiece
to her; she sucks life from the tank as you exhale,
and the panic begins; the test of trust
before she surrenders life back to you;
she points up, and you slowly rise, sharing air,
surrounded by the shining bubbles of your liability,
rising toward that distant sun,
breaking the surface together.

Moon, Ruins, Mykonos

Yasoo, she laughs, this hard wind
will cancel your trip to Mykonos, as I try
to understand the mad woman of the Plaka,
her souvlakia and beer, the Hotel Byron,
the East German alarm clock,
her Acropolis burning in the night sky;
but how to meet her? And what do I do
with all that beauty? I melt with the light
into the distance;

good night, Athena!
Kali nikta, my sweet princess!
I did love her pale ruins shining in the dark,
those old bones thrusting against the sky,
a white goddess lost in black hilarity;
kali nikta. I was the moon, lost, staring, outside,
wandering those starlit streets, that labryrinth
filled with bright shadows, windy silence,
dark corridors and white holes,
wide stones leading nowhere.

I was her lost child, a bright anchor
of refuse and pastel, lost alley ways
and buffeting sea, keyholes to a modern ruin.
The wind followed me,
a figure receding, waves crashing on the terrace,
my love lurking in the narrow doors,
hiding in the crowded sky, her
white dust clinging to the night.

Flogging the Glass

        The parents retire to a condo in Lake Worth,
still hooked to Florida,
filter feeders and key lime pie—
and all of it comes together, hissing
into crushed and polished shell, sunbleached histories,
translucent crabs collected on a gold coast,
piling sand on top of darker sand. They
won't talk about their parents, in Homestead,
West Palm Beach, Fort Lauderdale;
who needs more pain? "Whatever you ask, I won't
answer," she says, still a girl locked in a closet by white trash.
Boynton Beach, Lantana, Hypoluxo, Manalapan, Boca Raton,
Pompano Beach, Vero Beach, Juno Beach, Jupiter, Loxahatchee,
anhinga, grouper, dolphin, and loggerheads, memories
surging in and out with the tide,
casurinas sighing from ages past, her father
hefting record snook, that smell of drying weed and rotting fish,
the lobster migration lines, covering that soft twitching abdomen
in a shell, afraid in cold, murky waters,
but fearlessly listening to the warm echoes, then cancer,
an angry death, a stream of red lights vanishing
off the end of a pier.
        Hey you, what are you doing here, fishing
in the Keys? You wind through Angelfish Creek, and hit the flats
at noon. A heron flaps up, the midday heat sinks down,
and the wake spreads back
through the mangroves. You anchor, set the lines
and watch the fishheads float by.
Barracuda stalk the snapper hiding in rock holes.
In the turtlegrass, nurseries of crab, shrimp,
filefish, anemone, puffers, trunkfish, pipefish,
seahorses, stars and cucumbers, a shallow world
refracted in patterns scalloped

by current, sun and sand, a salty, shifting network
dancing in waves of light, caves
where orange crawfish hide their nervous
tails, those meaty abdomens, spasmodic,
clutching to the bottom, carapace stroked
with antennae in a decapod dalliance,
clicking, fizzing, buzzing, photo
synthesizing in a few feet of water,
a liquid desert, light beams arcing
in that emerald translucence you left to breathe air,
skirting the reef, dead brain coral, needlefish
cluttering your memory of the perfect silent alien world.
        The dark, low islands hold their secrets; their red roots
arch in a gray oolite wall. Fiddler crabs and hermits scuttle
through the black muck and ooze, rustling
among the rusty mangrove leaves, lost
among those arching, island-making roots.
You click claws in delight—
You are chileped news;
in your dreams you scuttle across those
ancient mangroves, a pair of purple claws,
or red, or blue, perhaps,
a most popular pet, a hermit crab
searching the ruddy night for a friendly tap
of the heavy chileped, the antennae quivering,
looking up to find yourself staring down
between arched roots. It's the merging of man
and crustacean, pods hugging the shore,
waiting to be replaced.
Bobbing in the current, you toss back a grunt,
watching it flash down to the cool bottom.
        She's the child who drinks her poison standing up,
who wills such sadness that bones moan and weep,

anchored in salt weeds not even summer tides can release,
this ocean of sweet skin, tart memories, tangy
surf breaking over teeth. What beach will comfort the dead,
or feed the most deserving? They moan not for release
but for a better wind; they struggle
in the golden yeast, a dying sea
of the brave and fallen. Her cloud sails on a velvet sea,
in terror — reaching for the wind
she begins the search again, as if beating back and forth
will clear away the fear of enclosure,
reaching for prey as she is hunted herself
by predators too large or small to see—
death will embarrass her, as a lingering scent
—such mean guidance from above,
the black wings, the yellow spawn
swept up onto the sand, above the tidal zone,
away from the reek of muck of decay
and muddy history, as the sun sets on Biscayne Bay;
Maybe it's just a chemical imbalance, an old memory,
the subtle growth of eyes and branches,
A sea hare, or nautilus, minding its own business,
The flatfish with the roving eye,
eroding with the brain buds still curled.
Yes, it all comes together, crashing into
sunbleached grains, past lives
settled for a time, after surging in and out with the tide,
from so many pasts, so many distant
lands that sigh with age, collected for a brief rest
after rushing around the globe. Life
piles on top of life, retired
to where she was born, fighting the uneducated cracker
to the end, while her father, the fishing engineer,
a Florida spiny lobster with a battery shack,

a broken marriage, and a lost career,
takes his daily dose of pain on Lake Worth Pier.
      Royal palms line Avocado Drive,
their fronds like proud plumes, marching off in columns
as the west clears at sunset; incandescent
cirrus clouds, pale and curled like faint wisps of hair,
sail slowly across the ruddy sky, promising fair weather;
fiddler crabs scuttle through tortured mangrove roots,
raising giant claws; we stumble along the Intra-Coastal
Waterway, through strangler figs and cabbage palms
at Gumbo Limbo, banded tropical spiders barring the way
with enormous perfect webs, and thousands of crabs rustling
in the rusty mangrove leaves, lost among those arching,
island-making roots, finding the crusty trail, and climbing
the look-out tower, above the green canopy,
swaying and alive, swaying and alive,
the whole world dancing in the warm sea breeze.

100% Miami

The door slams again
as if to say, get outside, die,
study the fire hydrant for clues;
get stoned again, something human,
buddy. Get along, buddy.
The doll says she prefers her damaged leg
and the ground drags me around.
The witch smiles,
Read boy, read this with lizard eyes,
don't look at the sun like a big ass
on sweaty cellophane.
Time drizzles
and I walk the plaza, protected by wet
clouds draped across
a cave of wriggling toes;
smell of coffee, urine, fresh-cut grass,
sixteenth summer,
shooting recipes for the sick ones.
My paint softens like
a sun-ripened mango, clinging
till it rots; I'm an old cracker
hugging the globe till someone
turns me into the lost.
I'm a river of spores
hunting new odors
in the golden air.

Gaia

I might as well call you Mother,
bare-breasted earth goddess
whose son dreams of barbed wire.
The shadow on the marble wall rises
through the centuries, walking through
the dust of scoured worshipped stone.
The gray heaven molds itself
into a whitewashed church on Mykonos,
a pale breast atop ragged rock,
black crosses poking through
the thin fabric that separates my dreams
from your sky; I melt into the Aegean
chasing ruins, rubbing raw the marble
skin, the boundaries of stiffened muscle,
agate eyes, floating south
into the empty blue towards Crete.
The glowing temple rocks to the beat
of the twentieth century, and fiery figures
dance in its shadows;
I must sleep now, and dream:
you're waving to the camera
in a yellow dress on a brown beach,
the ashes waiting for the sea. I kiss
your damaged flesh, smelling
the distant islands.

Do Miss the Cormorant

She hunts in the sound
below a slick surface
a sweet
insistent reek
of decay and fossil fuel
flowing endlessly
with the tides
Spreading her wings
on a beach
her sour coat of dark feathers
dries above the crude tar
of high water
Wind beats pale grass
flat into hard salt
shallow roots
baking transparent
white in the sun
The oil tanker bleeds offshore
her bitter iridescence
lapping the sand
in small black waves

The House that Jack Built

My parents tell me they're selling the house I grew up in
as we walk along the trail lined with ironwood, pine and fir
that leads to the end of Jack London's dream.
We come to a picket fence surrounding a large lava rock
the color of rust, the grave of America's first millionaire
author. Above us the branches of a big madrone
sag peacefully, peeling layers of dark red skin
that hang against the bright green. Ahead
through the redwood grove lie the charred ruins
of Wolf House, where tall thin chimneys of rust-red stone climb
into the bare blue sky like tough temple columns,
perched on that perfect slope like a stubborn argument.
As my parents talk about the homes they grew up in,
I see Charmian's House of Happy Walls;
I see the Valley of the Moon,
and Jack's dream house burning,
and Jack riding a tractor just before his death;
I see my mother and father
with me always; I see the red dust swirling
into the past, an old iron tractor
rusting in the green woods.

Happy Anniversary at Suicide Bridge

Maryland's Eastern Shore assails the nose
with 400 years of fecundity and farms,
intimate, ancient odors that trail us from town to town,
the sweet stench of crab and corn, cow and compost,
rotting fish and wild onion, freshcut garlic,
and clapboard homes on cinder blocks,
and old boats dissolving in tall fields.
We celebrate five years of marriage,
searching blackwater wilds for birds of prey,
and then searching for food ourselves,
as the sun sets on Cheseapeake Bay;
cicadas scream. Each moment is a loss, and we fear,
not darkness, not the cold, exactly, but the twilight
reminders that we're one year closer to the answer.
We drive past Cambridge to Suicide Bridge Restaurant,
near the Choptank River; fat green caterpillars
crawl slowly in the road. We see winter
in a spider's face on Suicide Bridge;
time is against us. We gaze longingly
at the bugeye, the skipjack, the schooner — old watercraft
still sailing, painfully clear on this fading autumn day.
Yellow poplars bleed red leaves, marsh grass spears the sky
with gold in the late fall sun, woods thinning but still rich
with green possibilities, with pathways and creeks
and sunlit spaces in a forest on fire.
We blind ourselves in the sun's molten track
on smooth current, our fears ebbing with the tide.

In and Out of Marin

After balancing frozen accounts you jump
into Marin County late at night, to join
the lovely engines searching
for Smash Palace, and you call on your
lunatic friends to watch the moon dim
and brighten like demented neon.
The best are dead, the rest too weary
but the dark fog rolls over the jeweled
Valley, glowing with its bazaar notions
while traffic spreads her loving arms
and lascivious legs. You wonder where
she went, squealing into the past;
you wonder if the highway beats
a wild lament, the rhythm of the roadsigns
here and then, the minutes piled along
the road to mock your progress
through the night.

Rehabilitation

When will we be saved, two cicadas
on distant trees,
two mannequins in separate window
beds, wet with surfing love, the future
crashing on the shore,
breath rippling in the hurricane of happiness,
the heaven and the hell that is us?

We listen to the fall we can't ignore;
when will you be ready, when will I,
the high wind blending our
flotsam on the sand, as we try again
these late September winds,
now threats, now promises, heartbendings,
like that time on Chincoteague Island,
when a boy spied on us.

We hunt for the missing skin of cicada,
shrill and empty spikes of sound,
the last days of sky filled with cicadas
settling down; our sluggish souls bang away—
little boy, will you go?

The end of summer makes us sob,
the scream of cicadas on a brass day,
whining for success with hours of life,
soaking up the sun, fat berries
shining on the vines, draped canopies
of ivy; each day is a loss, and we fear fall,
as the sky darkens.

We agree the day has been
sickeningly beautiful, a waste, you know,
so clear you could see spiders miles away,
their webs glistening bravely,
their gift-wrapped prey hanging heavily
among the pokeweed.

Another Van Gogh

Your bright colors spread their liquid fingers
Through the lonely blades of grass
Flashing beneath the searing sun like spears of gold
Friendless, you stalk the light with hopeless
Love, your sky blue eyes staring
From out of their dark clouds as the sun rains
And there is no escape; the light dissolves,
Flowing through the sweet skin of the earth,
And the parched plant flowers only once,
Surrounded by the blond sands
And the empty sky. Your love flies broken
Through the air, too dry to touch, fingers of light
Stretching in an orange arc that reaches me
As from ancient muscles glimmering;
What once was less than news
Is now beyond praise; and I have chosen
Words to exist, almost as I have chosen you.
This love endures, like the ragged workers
Cringing in the green heat; like the wind shrieking
As you shove the earth closer to the sun,
Searching for the yellow image with compound eyes;
Ah, Vincent, you golden ghost
Rushing through the bones of rain,
Sinking in the endless grass,
How often must I repeat your failures?
Your love stares at me through the pulsing bruise
Of a tormented light, a bright blue skin
Too proud in a dry history.

Cicada

You think you're more to me
than I am to you! But I'll burrow
under your soil
for another seventeen years,
buried in the past
but ringing in your memory like a plague
of love and hate,
and after all those years, like magic,
I'll crawl out again
and hook on a pine tree,
sucking sap, clawing a cicada tune,
humming a few shrill bars
that you'll remember,
a love song resonating
at the core of your loneliness.
Summer lost, I'll shriek and hiss,
and you'll miss me again,
for I have crawled these
seventeen summers to the surface
to break out my wings
and die in one last skin,
our brief passion spent,
splitting the wet,
hot night with a buzzing curse,
devoured at last.

Ground Zero

Red stripes shiver in the fetid breeze,
vultures get down on their knees,
crows strut and fret upon the stage,
the old man shouts in rage
at her lovely, delicate remains,
blossoming in black pain.

A big fireball erupts, engines scream,
and nothing is what it seems.
All has been taken from them, the feel
of summer sun burning skin as they reel
and fall, all they might say, frail
deeds that might dance in a green bay.
We have fears that we will always be
this way, a warm sun, a clear blue sky,
the few clouds, oblivious as white cats,
drifting by, then disappearing in ash.

We are incomplete survivors, with eyes
not blinded by the big surprise;
the big red ball melts and squeezes down
through all those bodies, to the ground.
Made fear-fresh, we have seen God,
but is He so important? Behold the cloud
of God's lament; the round red
cough explodes and scatters in blood
and dust — bodies vaporize, a blend
of shattered lives and molten
steel, that suffocating smell
clogging the fetid air, the gritty hell
of bent metal and fallen stone,
crumbled in a pile like broken bones.

In what was the 37th floor
we find the last full measure
of devotion, a blackened corpse,
charred and fragile as our hopes.

But evolution is too slow, and
heavy tanks race over the sand
with red stripes flying, the old man
shouting madly at the sun.
Oh endless road, endless road we run
To find and fight the enemy again.

Code Seven Seven

Before your shift began, late that afternoon,
you saw your first autopsy, each organ
carefully weighed--the innocent heart
alone on a shelf, the "brain barrel"
filled with cortex bobbing in formaldehyde.
Now, hours later, you're on your last call
of the night; you're a transportation orderly, in ICU.
Outside the window, a light snow falls;
but in this small glass room, the air
is thick and humid with decay, like a greenhouse.
The burn patient stares up at you,
a Code Seven Seven waiting to happen, only
his eyes moist, the remains of his skin not real,
the raw flesh exposed, red and yellow layers
from bark to core, tubes and wires dangling
like plastic vines, the charred roots of toes like coal.
He shivers while you sweat through the mask.
The nurse returns to change the sheets.
"Turn him towards you," she says. "A half roll.
Let's clean this up." You hold him on his side,
his good hand gripping your arm.
The snow has stopped, the night is clear;
a radiator knocks, a monitor whines.
A loudspeaker hisses into life.

Pain

Mrs. Tibbet fell thirty feet and landed
on a weathervane, and her pain flew
like an eagle toward the blinding sun
before plunging into drugs and mind
less pastimes. Mrs. Ruth Tibbet
heard voices calling her to China,
calling her to hug the breast of God
and pass out pamphlets named in honor
of the chosen dead. Ruth divorced
her faithless husband, joined
the local health club, screamed at no
one, felt no paean of purpose, shopped
for vitamins and nephews, helped
preserve the body politic and held
her head the way giraffes do,
munching on the crowns of trees. Ruth
answered every plea for money, every
call for sin. She drank a lot of
juice, sang at church, and remarried,
an older man who was dean
of women at the Universal Life College.

Desafinado

America, the stars are draped across
your broken bridges,
your back rests in the sea
and twilight's purple bruise
lies in your eyes. Your blue lights
are pills for a dusk
just too serene, the city remains
just out of range. We call to all our
hungry clay children, rise and grin
and kiss the fat man's hand;
the pudgy fingers grip the switch.
Bare trees crack the sky;
you dash around like a frightened bird.
When it's warmer we can live off the land
but now it's better to stay inside.
Old man, with your snowy hair
and smiling cracks, soon we will be
all light. No gun, no fun. But he prays
for the undead; they are a team
at night, but the guns keep jamming
as he chases the undead
Clay People, who say, Keep it up, baby,
indulge, it's the American Way. OK,
so what does he owe them,
a thousand clay zombies
struggling to high ground
through broken TV sets, couches and mud,
the long, slow walk of the undead,
guided by streams of red velvet?
Why don't they dig a rut of their own,
plant themselves in the same soil,

get buried in the same ground, wriggling
around in the mud, to freshen up for spring?
They are beautiful, those undead,
and he follows them, surrounded
by a crowd of guns, pounding
to the beat of the future.

The Arena

The bus engine, naked under the back
seat, grinds and whines in my
ears, roars in my eyes as I drift
to work groaning in the morning commute.
Suddenly I'm in the arena, and the stands
are booing, the crowd standing, giving
the thumbs down.
Death to the poet. But then a voice
saves me — it is my
lover — no, it's the bus driver
waking me up; we've arrived at the terminal.
I join the separate fleshes
flowing out of the station, faces
like paper clips wrapped in gray.
I walk out into the arena.

American Movie Classics

My love goddess,
my Rita — I was fifty years too late!
The train to Istanbul
has left, and you have given up on me.
The love you wanted wasn't meant to be—
or had you picked me from the fantasies
of your love god — and then I had to say,
"The train is approaching the border,
Rita, flick on the lights!
It's time to escape!"
Rita, you're covered in mink,
dragging yourself through the woods
on one bad leg, shouting at strangers,
searching for the glamour
that never dies.
Up ahead, you hear the echo of the city
Carnival, the city of mirrors
where you will be saved.

Moon Dog

Maybe it's just because I'm sad,
but I look at this fat moon rising
and think of it as mine,
my very own orange light
sitting on the Richmond Bridge,
and I walk my old dog with a torn gray heart,
following *my* moon through *my* trees,
the small dog sniffing
at every bush, every shadow on the ground.
So let my orange light fall
on this old terrier; let him drink
my moonshine — it's going to swallow *him*
soon, anyway. Next,
he starts rolling around in the leaves.
Come on, pal, that's not impressive;
can't you fly?
I let him make one last circle
around his world, guarding his master's land,
a star-gazer and an overgrown rodent
exploring their twilight together.
You proud descendent
Of the wolf, the jackal,
you growling manipulator, filled
with human need! You live a human's life,
knowing the lie, knowing
you're a hairy reflection, a canine alter ego,
here to dress up *my* loneliness,
a shaggy shadow on a Sunday night,
a companion for the evening Moon Walk.
My old friend has almost outlived his welcome
in this life,
exulted by the flowers, a sniffing,

twitching pup grown old, beyond his time—
but he looks at me eagerly,
in a private dog heaven! He's tough enough
to be my best friend,
if I was really doing something
worthwhile; his shadow pauses suddenly
in my moonlight, to mark his territory,
like his owner still filled with the urge to say,
This is mine.

The Chapel of Memories

You drag me up at night,
lift me over the city,
past the pool of the dead
where we smell the breath
of restless souls like jasmine
floating in the mist;
we drift past the couple
with no faces
glowing in the fog;
we rise over the columbarium,
past the Payless, the Safeway,
high above the undulating lights
of San Francisco;
we sail through a night sky
like a warm sea of candles.

Sea Drums

Wood bends to storm, would rather dance
on waves — which craft is faster — mine
or my progenitors — there is a chance
to make peace, to rig, to sail blind

And in my wake is their wake—
And ahead — but am I so far behind?
There's no horizon, no ship, no break
Between sea and sky; alone I find

No burning clouds. I stretch and press
With wind, and laugh, and then release
And when she quits I smell the past,
And grab the life lines, and try to splice

the frayed ends, but the sails will tear;
the sea, the wake, will always be there.

All Advice is Bad; Good Advice is Fatal

And children tumble in the front door
and what ground shall the birdsongs cover?
The green tree covers
what ground and what ground
shall the fresh earth cover?
We wait, and the time is short
but the waiting is long;
in the old house there is always listening
and more is heard than spoken
and what is spoken remains in the room
waiting for the future to hear it;
and whatever happens began in the past
and presses hard on the future—
the agony in the curtained bedroom
where someone's thought of dying
gathers into itself all the voices of the past
and projects them into the future,
the treble voices on the lawn
(something about hay in summer;
the dogs and the old pony
stumble in pain).
Is it the chopping of wood in autumn
and the singing in the kitchen
and the steps at night in the corridor,
the moment of sudden loathing,
the season of stifled sorrow,
the whisper, the transparent deception,
the keeping up of appearances,
the making the best of a bad job?
There is no avoiding these things
and we know nothing of exorcism,
and whether in Argus or England

there are certain inflexible laws,
unalterable in nature's music;
there is nothing at all to be done about it;
there is nothing to do about anything
and now it is nearly time for the news;
we must listen to the weather report
and the international catastrophes.

Reasons for Breathing

She was searching for the trades,
endlessly hungering
for those wings
again, and her sails
have become my skin.
Whitecaps dragged my craft
to leeward, toward a glittering fleet
of ghosts that lies offshore,
rich with sunset palms
and burning clouds in late day.
I caught up with my past,
hiding off that distant isle,
recovering from faulty navigation;
I skirted reef,
a blur of might-have-beens
and almost-weres, dropped sails
and anchor, dragging;
the weight was good
but soon I drifted free,
hit smooth water, under red sky,
just one thin layer separating us,
and I exulted, and despaired your
greater endurance,
inhaling the last smell.

Now the sea's a bruise
that inhales light,
celebrating the wreck
of youthful fools.
I struggle against the tide
of my mother's blood,
choking through the current,
the beaches hissing

in the dark, scratching
the swell, her auburn hair
as white now as a bow wave—
my mother's hull, her pale lips
pressed to my cynical skin,
her loose sheets,
the gentle wail of water
entering, the hush of wind
leaving the sail—

I search the indigo horizon,
surf pounding the reef,
her lost child wandering
near the edge of the sky,
the sailor, the explorer, the fool—
She dreams that I am one of them,
bound for home on a voyage
still inside of her, discovering her,
finding my albatross still soaring
over the imagined land;
it will end where it began,
the warm breeze of her sigh,
her love rising like a fresh wind
—where have you been—
After all those promises
of bright days on the green bay,
white caps dancing,
but all is still now, flat
in the dying breeze, lovely craft
anchored in azure.

The Landlady and the Fireman

Old Mrs. Brady munches nuts.
She says her gas pains
Hurt worse than childbirth.
Nothing is worth that.
Her eyes dampen
As she cites her grandson's
Latest crimes.
He's in the Home again.
Fog peers in the windows.
Sunset slashes
Through the alleys
Across small plots of lawn.
The unread bookcase dims.
Her husband's portrait blurs
Atop The Newlywed Game.
No one parks
On her black strip of drive.
The fireman will never return
To take the place of pills.
All around her perfect parlor
Ancient ashes seem to settle.

Bad Day at Skull Rock

I reach for frozen sun,
a yucca standing in a sea of sand,
my blades flashing at nothing
in the green air,
and grow tall, staring
at the children;
circling in black circles
on a white day, they drift down
on one-room apartments;
they pick at the remains
of Skull Rock;
what are you looking for
in the face of the dead,
I'm asking now
but the sun burns through me
and streams along the dark valleys.

Loss of Immunity in San Francisco

Thick dark fog surrounds the Sutro Tower
like a sea of Friday nights, but this
good night is soon to end; I see dawn
stalking in your eyes, but your thin
face is calm now, free of all surprises.
While the rest of Noe Valley sleeps
we read poems, talk of deconstruction,
Wallace Stevens, final disabilities.
I see you marching from your distant
citadel in the fog, through a forest
of placid trees grown thick with lichen.
Across the bay I see the gray missiles
of the Mormon Temple, where city lights
still blaze in silent fury. Stubborn,
proud, they blanket the rolling hills
like brilliant minds, so endless once,
now one by one departing with the dawn.

Bag Lady

I see you all over town,
because the city talks to you.
You're an avatar of the city's lost,
a riddle with two legs and a shopping cart.
Your power flows from that bag; it's seen the town
from top to bottom. The riddle runs through tunnels and
saxophones, through you, in old bags in a world of terminal
commuters. You're an avatar of re-use, and redemption.
You hide your secrets in that bag, the death angels of
recycling. How many lost dreams could you
release, to spread through town and run
the streets? Those sympathetic sounds
are repeated daily in the goodyear
house, but there's nothing else
to do; it's a place to do business, they
rub you the right way in this house, under
water, the Third and Howard alcoholics. You
have almost graduated, a carnival of burnt oranges,
a raw wound, a smile that reminds me of plastic brace
lets on charred brown skin. Bracelets with your name and
the hospital, the only face I trust, something other than sympathy.
In the wet cold December, sleeping alone off the subway,
you don't ask for a hand to throw green stuff in the air,
wads of doughy smiles floating down and scattering.
You watch hands flutter like pigeons to clutch
posterity, dim memories of cars and frigidairs,
clutched by a dirty palm, a mouth that opens
to the whine of traffic, smirking, rushing
home, an old town with young diseases,
a season of fighting for your gray
terrain, an angry bruise, a dirty
arm, a bloody fist shoved in
your face; you're a salvation
Santa, clutching your bag
of gifts, the rub of Ham
let, the spirit of Christ
mas in paper or plastic.

How May We Help You

Thank you for calling this giant corporation
Your call is important to us
So we will not answer the phone
And we will force you to listen to show tunes
And push useless buttons for hours
And we will keep you waiting
And we may finally get you a live
Person who will promptly pass you off to
Another person who will send you back
To the first person so she can cut you off
So you can call again, and again, and wait
—How are we doing?
Did you expect our staff to give a damn?
Did you wait patiently for someone?
—Did you have to wait more than 5 hours?
Did you think you were entitled to service?
—Thanks for your patience!
Did you get any useful information at all?
Do you think we care?
What the hell did you want?
—Your call is important to us!
If you believe that you got grits for brains
Do you think we want to improve our service?
—Would you like a personal response?
We get millions of calls, you silly fart!
—We're sorry, but we do not show any record of that
transaction in this
department. *Maybe their system is down. Please*
call back later.

And keep calling until somebody cares!
—*Please call back during office hours.*
Yeah, we know it's office hours now,
but we got better things to do, so piss off.
OK, leave your name and number and hold your breath
—*Thanks for playing!*
Thank you for helping us waste *your* time!
—*Is there anything else we can help you with today?*

He Has Seen God

Well, now we have virtual redemption—
Some lovely, virtual towers of data
    Some new cells and some memory loss—
The merger of Satan and Spiderman,
    Fuzzy cells hugging the globe
Waiting to be activated and replaced
    We are fragile children in flight
Caught in the awful velocity
    Of time, a thick column of smoke rising on the wind—
As we listen to the virtual news, more cyber life, more
    Virtual misery—
Fear is the price we pay for freedom
    But we've been there before—
We say our little prayers
    And take our little pill
And think of all the bastards
    We really want to kill
So let us go then, you and I
    When the evening drops from the sky
Like towers collapsing into dust
    And it is time to turn around again
(We won't tell you what information
    We want from you but
Things are all right, hate crouches in the rocks
    Afraid its shadow will spill
Into daylight sand, and be found out
    Thankfully life is a mumble and a blur—
The fault, dear Cassius, is not in our stars
    But in our cells, as users.)
Having read *Transcendentalism for Dummies*,
    Chuck gets the Word from Mount Sign-on;
"He has seen God," says Yvonne:
    Thou shall have no other Gates before me;

Honor thy Windows and thy Upgrades;
     Thou shall not take the name MicroSoft in vain;
Thou shall not hack, or suffer virus;
     Thy memory shall not download or spawn external views
If there is not enough disk space—
     Thou shall not pirate thy neighbor's software;
The NRA shall inherit the earth—
     Moses! Save us! And discover how easy it is to
YOUR MESSAGE HAS PERMANENT
     FATAL ERRORS
THIS PROGRAM HAS PERFORMED
     AN ILLEGAL OPERATION AND WILL
BE SHUT DOWN
     IF THE PROBLEM PERSISTS, CONTACT
THE PROGRAM VENDOR
     "So let it be written. And the silver cord is cut
from the old earth. Amen."
     Now, get thee down!
Thy files have corrupted themselves!
     Don't know what
Life is — indeed, life is
     Only for the future—
Not enough disk space for the past
     Backup Files Lost—
A device attached to the system / is not functioning
     Genetic flaws are not our fault—
Child of the Universe Cosmic Hotline,
     Keep looking up, may we help you?
Our special guests tonight are
     Bill Gates, Chuck Heston, and Jehovah—
Like sweating tourists and antiseptic nymphs
     We feel bare, like Moses gazing
From Mount Pisgah to the Promised Land

Nada Mas

I fear your archaic smile
Arches dipping into the beach
A feral scent rising on the sea breeze
The lingering cicada death rattle
The webbed paws and spider love
Frozen webs glistening like tears
Like viscous stars
The merging leaf and bagworm
The snow is catching me—
My hair is faded, defiant crystals
Frozen foam
A surf storm of white water
I fear your ancient laugh
Echoing through tortured roots
Scratching lips and lapping ripples
Frozen with a dusting of snow
Whose parents have I passed
Endlessly waking
Whose progeny
Weary of the search
The scream of crickets
The cheers of the decomposed
Surrendering to water
Your warm hands running
On my mad skin
Just outside the sea lanes
Just beyond the fringe
The surf traffic
What else do I fear
Survival is an ugly bird
Poking in the cinders
Bred amidst the burning

O Lord, we prey
On Thee, the reek
Of Thy purity
That coileth in charred flesh
We swallow hair and feathers
We burn with the love
Of all breeders — we choke
With love, my sweet progenitors
On the thick white lint of snow
Trees blaze with early sun
Before low clouds shut it all down
Soon after dawn
Sunrise struggles through white crystals
Burning limbs and needles
Bronze columns surly, glowing
Why are people here?
Your parents are dead.
Thrown in reverse
We must end this
Progress

Mientras el Hombre la Admira y la Vulnera

From the jungle floor her soft limbs
of brown stone rise through green light
while man admires and wounds

A thousand years of sun have burned away
the bright plumes of the feathered serpent
the jaguar and the eagle

No matter; rain still dances on Mayan walls
and a young woman still opens
to love; as firm, as yielding

as the yellow acacia petals dripping
in the rain, lost in the Yucatan
mientras el hombre la admira y la vulnera

Her people wear white dresses
dissolving in her charred soil
melting in her porous limestone

Her smile shines like white sand
baking in the sun; iguanas race across
her tiled surface

A thousand years of storms have risen
to a hushed expectancy; winds and rain
chase away the heat

The sky cools now, thunder cracking open
her dark heart filled with red flowers
her breath hisses with musty lovers

The bubbling calls of small children rise
from inside her overgrown temples
where no children play

Her mouth is a dry pool in blue shade
skin crumbling beautifully
ancient droppings older than death

Smoke rises in the still fetid air
from the rubble of Uxmal and Chichen Itza
while man admires and wounds

Her eyes are black chambers filled with madness
bees and swallows trying to escape
mientras el hombre la admira y la vulnera

Bert J.Hubinger,

born in New Jersey and raised in Florida, has traveled the land and sea in search of adventures in sailing, diving, and maritime history. With degrees from Dartmouth College and Catholic University, he is a teacher, an editor, a photographer, and a frequent contributor to a variety of publications.

♦

"Hubinger's writing provides a passport to the soul's richest ports. He knows nature's most intimate details and treats them with the respect of a consummate and appreciative lover."
—*Mitzi Mabe, Professor of Writing, University of Maryland*

"The original and appealing voice in *Sea Drums & Other Poems* tempts the reader into a world of contrasts. His poems take us to a place where water meets the shore and irony meets the literal."
—*Susan Rosen, author of* ShoreWords

"With surreal image and droll metaphor, Hubinger's savvy word choice and admirable economy of words expand to a view of the 20th century. From poignant narrative to lyrical satire, each poem brings the reader into its world immediately. His spectrum of subjects is broad. Hubinger's imagination and rich detail bring reality its dream in poetry."
—*Jacklyn W. Potter, Director, Joaquin Miller Cabin Poetry Series*

ISBN 1-885457-50-2

50995

9 781885 457509

ROSEBUD PRESS
Imprint of
EASTWIND PUBLISHING
Annapolis & Trappe, Maryland

$9.95